Speak It Now!

Speak It Now!

Affirmations
for
Self-Care   Self-Love   Self-Worth

Dr. La'Vel F. Hardy

XULON PRESS

Xulon Press
2301 Lucien Way #415
Maitland, FL 32751
407.339.4217

www.xulonpress.com

ISBN-13: 978-1-6628-1413-6

Table of Contents

Dedication

I dedicate this book to my husband, Rexsell Hardy. Thank you for encouraging me to be all that I can be and more.

A special thanks to my children, Rexsell, Jasmine, and Tiffany, for honoring me with the title of mom.

I cherish my grandchildren, Rexsell III and Reign, for being my heartbeats.

I am grateful for my foundation; my parents, Elgin and Velma Little; and my grandmother, Bessie Botto, for teaching me life's lessons.

Thank you to God's House of All Nations church for your support and love.

I pay homage to Bishop Ernestine Cleveland Reems for being a trailblazer for women in ministry.

Introduction

This book was birthed out of joy, excitement, encouragement, love, pain, hurt, tears, disappointment, and life lessons.

As my life has progressed, I have learned how important it is to take charge and speak over my life. I speak wholeness, wellness, and healing over my body, my mind, my heart, and the air I breathe. Therefore, I speak and apply positive affirmations over every aspect of my journey.

As you read this book along your walk of life, begin to speak these affirmations daily, and the words you speak will soon transform your life.

I hope this book encourages you to understand your voice and allow your spoken words to take root in your life. You will not lose your voice, but your voice will have power to reset your mind and heart.

Preface

As a child, I grew up in a well-balanced home, with parents and a grandmother who were my number-one encouragers. My grandmother was always reading and learning. Her theory was: "You are never too old to learn."

Well, I never adapted to that theory. I did not like school, especially reading. However, I always lived my life to please my parents and grandmother, and it has become clear to me that reading is necessary and fundamental.

I decided to finish school and make my family proud. This goal enabled me to complete and obtain the following degrees: Associate's, Bachelor's, Master's, and Doctorate.

I hope everyone who has been afforded the opportunity to read this book will be encouraged to keep pressing on, pushing forward, and persevering. Giving up is not an option.

I want this book to empower all to live a better life as you travel the road to best. Everyone's life is worth living, and every person has the power to change the placement and assignment of their life.

This book represents my highs and lows in life. I have learned to encourage myself and speak life over and into my story. Throughout my life, these affirmations have encouraged me to be a better version of myself.

My Happy Place

When I am happy with myself, my demeanor and my actions will represent where I am in life.

This phase of life indicates that no matter what is going on in the present, I have made the choice to always smile.

I will be genuinely happy with myself and by myself.

I will not depend on anyone or anything to make me happy.

I will create my happy space, and my smile will be genuine.

I smile because I can!

Peace, Not Pieces

Romans 12:18
If it be possible, as much as lieth in you,
live peaceably with all men.

I must make the decision not to live amongst chaos. I will surround myself with calm and peace.

I will live in peace, not pieces.

I will not allow my atmosphere and environment to become contaminated, tainted, or poisonous.

One day at a time, I will transform my life to completion and wholeness.

IT IS BETTER WE DISINTEGRATE IN PEACE AND NOT IN PIECES.

Calm Amid Desperation

Isaiah 55:8-9

8. For my thoughts are not your thoughts, neither are your ways my ways, saith the Lord.

---

9. For as the heavens are higher than the earth, so are my ways higher than your ways, and my thoughts than your thoughts.

I will not rush the process of Life.

Amid desperate situations, I will take time to think, consider, and reconsider.

I will savor every minute that I have been blessed to live.

I pray daily that my thoughts and ways line up with those of God.

Who Am I?

I am essential!

I am necessary!

I am important!

I am loved!

Therefore, my life has value, worth, and purpose.

Accepting Ownership

I will own my every failure.

I will own every facet of my life.

I will smile at every victory.

I will embrace every accomplishment.

It's Okay Not to Be Okay

I am not a perfect person.

I have learned how to accept the various paths of my life.

I have faced moments of despair, but I did not succumb to them.

It's okay not to be okay, and admit it.

EVERYTHING WILL
BE OKAY
IN THE END
IF IT'S
NOT OKAY
IT'S NOT
THE END

Life's Decisions

While on the pathway of life, I will either attract
or grant access to things and people.

I will make a conscious decision to accept
or deny them.

As I go through life, my actions, ways,
friendships, and relationships will connect me to those
who deserve to have me in their life.

I will take myself off discount, for my worth
has just increased.

Breaths of Life

Genesis 2:7
And the Lord God formed man of the dust of the ground and breathed into his nostrils the breath of life; and man became a living soul.

I am worth every breath I breathe!

I will value and cherish every day as if it is my last.

I will not waste my breath on things that have the potential to decrease my life's value.

Word Power

Proverbs 11:17
Your own soul is nourished when you
are kind, but you destroy yourself when
you are cruel.

I've got this.

I have the power to speak those things that be not,
as though they were.

I will be victorious and successful, and I will live
a fulfilled life.

Seeing with Clarity

Proverbs 16:24
Pleasant words are as an honeycomb,
sweet to the soul, and health to the bones.

I am empowered, enlightened, and encouraged.

There is nothing that will defy my inner power.

I will change my prescription, and my vision will become clearer.

I will look at my life through the lens of clarity.

Faith and Feet

Romans 10:17
So, then faith cometh by hearing, and hearing by the word of God.

A goal without a plan is simply a wish.

My goals will have intent and depth so that I can secure their placement in my life.

I will fine tune my life's goals and put feet to my faith.

My goals will come into fruition.

You are the author of your life

I See Me

Proverbs 18:21
Death and life are in the power of the tongue: and they that love it shall eat the fruit thereof.

I am valued!

I matter!

I am worth it!

When I look in the mirror, I see what matters

Me!

I'm Not my Hair
I'm Not my Skin
I am the
Soul,
that lives within

Me First

I will value my personal life over my professional life.

I will care for, tend to, love, and nurture those special qualities within me that make me who I am and what I am!

Change does not come by chance; it comes by choice.

Therefore, I will make my choices count.

All that matters is that I am alive and I live!

Stress-Free

1 Peter 3:10
For he that will love life, and see good days, let him refrain his tongue from evil, and his lips that they no speak guile:

I give myself permission to live a stress-free life.

I will not let situations over which I have no control overwhelm me.

Nothing has access to my life unless I grant it permission.

I will keep my atmosphere and environment free from anything that is capable of taking me to a dark place.

Choices of Life

God has given us the opportunity to make choices for our life. Your choices will come with either rewards or consequences.

Write down what you choose to be in your life:

I Choose to Be:

_____   _____
_____   _____
_____   _____
_____   _____
_____   _____
_____   _____
_____   _____
_____   _____
_____   _____
_____   _____

Circle of Life

I will take care of myself first, then consider everybody else.

I am no longer second.

I cannot be an asset if I allow myself to become a liability to myself or others.

I am a proud specimen that God has created.

My life will come full circle.

Game Changer

My life is a best seller.

All who are connected to me value my life.

I have planted and watered seeds that have been game changers.

I will travel the road called "Better,"
which will lead me to my best.

My Greatest Investment

I am my greatest investment.

I will be my greatest encourager.

I will reassure myself daily that I was created with
the tenacity and the strength of God.

I will recognize who I am and whose I am.

Wholeness of Life

I am mentally whole.
I will guard my mind and tend to every thought that
has gained entry.
My thoughts and ideas are housed in my mind,
so I will ensure my think tank is cleared of
excessive baggage.

I am emotionally whole.
I will allow myself to experience all emotions.
I will not stay in a mind space that causes me to
operate in a paranoid state of mind.
I will be conscious of feelings that have the tendency
to psychologically damage me.

I am physically whole.
I will always listen to my body when it talks to me,
and not wait until it screams at me.
My body represents the wholeness of my life.

SELF care

IS NOT SELFISH

Knowing My Placement

I care about who I am and what I am.

Self-care is setting boundaries.

People may be my priority, but I may not be theirs.

I have learned to accept my placement in the lives of others.

Better Days Ahead

May each new day prove to be better in every
aspect of my life.

My life will be better each day because my mindset
has changed the direction of the paths that I travel.

I will continue to search my life and know I am not
at the end of it.

Better is the next step to the best of my life.

The Real

I won't start healing until I stop pretending.

I will stop pretending to be happy.

I will stop pretending to be free from my past.

I will stop pretending to have all the answers about my life.

I will stop pretending that all is perfect.

I will put down phony and pick up real.

I will not live my life to please others.

I will accept who I am and what is beneficial to advancing me toward the best of my life.

I will no longer operate under fear of the unknown.

One Moment in Time

My present is just one moment in time, and I will not allow this moment to hold me hostage.

Moments in my life seem to have longevity, but I must remember a moment is only a brief period of time.

I will go ahead and free myself.

COLLECT *moments* NOT THINGS

Life's Seasons

Every season comes with good and bad.

Every season has its likes and dislikes, depending on one's preferences.

Every season has its pros and cons.

Seasons can vary significantly in their characteristics.

The passing of a season can bring changes to my atmosphere and environment.

The ending of a season is a sign that there is another season to follow.

I will make a conscious decision to dissect every season in order to produce positive results.

I am amid a life-changing, mind-resetting, and life-altering season.

Season of Winter

Winter Represents:
Cold weather
Snow (depending on one's location)
Shorter days
Trees with no leaves
Green grass that has turned brown
Icy conditions
Warm dress code
Joyful holidays
In my season of winter, I will learn how to
adapt to the changes of winter.

I must learn:

- The appropriate attire needed to handle life's temperature changes
- how to handle the times when I must confront some dead things.
- what to do when the sun does not always shine.
- what to do when dark days seem to outweigh the bright days.
- during the winter, there are some good days that bring along smiles and cheerfulness.

Season of Spring

Spring Represents:
Temperatures slowly rising
Increased rainfall
Cold and dark dwindling away
Light beginning to shine bright
Trees beginning to grow their leaves
Fresh buds blooming
Animals awakening
Seeds being planted
Seeds taking root
Vegetation growing
Snow from the previous season melting

In my season of spring, I will experience:

- new beginnings.
- new life.
- the transition between changing temperatures.
- bouncing back.
- new adventures.
- dead things coming back to life.
- always being ready for the rain or drought.
- rejuvenation.

Spring can be an inviting and feel-good season.

Season of Summer

Summer Represents:
Weather increasing to its hottest
Probability of heatwaves
Droughts occurring
Flowers in full bloom
Grass being green or brown, depending on
how you tend to it

This season opens the opportunity for
many activities.

This season is considered a peak time in society.

Even in this season, there are people who
prefer the cooler climates.

In the season of summer, we have the opportunity
to travel and enjoy water sports.

I will not allow life's heat to consume me.

I will be vigilant of the possibility of drought.

I will always be prepared for life's heatwaves that
have capabilities of draining me.

I will tend to life so that it will flourish and
be healthy.

Season of Fall

Fall Represents:
Weather becoming cooler
Plants becoming dormant
Leaves transitioning to many colors
Tree shedding their leaves
Birds beginning to leave certain climates
Crisp leaves replacing flowers
Animals preparing for winter

This is my season of ripeness and maturity.

I will reap in this season of harvest.

In this season, I will enjoy the residue of the previous season.

Fall has the tendency to be a comforting time.

I will enjoy every moment of calm.

I will prepare for the next season by gathering the necessary apparatuses needed for my transition.

Loving Me

Loving myself more enables me to love others despite our differences.

My love is unconditional.

My love is limitless.

My love is genuine.

Love Yourself First

Because that's who you'll be spending the rest of your life with

Living a Satisfied Life

I will stop complaining and learn to live life with what I have.

I will be content, but I will always strive toward excellence.

My life is what I make of it.

I will live and enjoy every moment and make the best of any situation to which I am privy.

A Work in Progress

I'm working on myself, for myself, and by myself.

The only one I have control over is myself.

Only I have the power to change myself.

Therefore, I will focus on every aspect of my life.

My Life's Story

A person cannot value me more than
I value myself.

When I cry, that is my life's story.

When I smile, that is my life's story.

When I am happy, that is my life's story.

When I am misunderstood, that is
my life's story.

When I am lonely, that is my life's story.

When I am frustrated, that is my life's story.

When my heart is broken, that is my life's story.

When I am victorious, that is my life's story.

I will recognize who I am and whose I am.

The Weight of My Strength

I did not know my own strength until it was all I had left.

I will not allow anything to consume me.

I will not allow anything to infiltrate my life, taking me off the course of positivity and excitement.

Staying Focused

Looking out the window allows me to see others, but this can sometimes be distracting.

I must not lose my focus. I must redirect my sight and learn to look deep into my life to examine the whole me.

I must acknowledge what I see and be willing to search and address all aspects of myself, whether good or bad.

stay focused
and
NEVER GIVE UP!

My Responsibility

I am not selfish; I am just in love with me.

I have allowed my life to be shifted in ways that have caused me to face consequences.

I have unconsciously allowed my life to spiral out of control.

I am taking my life back.

I will accept total responsibility and love the total me.

The Higher Power

I will live my life on purpose.

My life has been guided by a higher power that is greater than me.

The power within me will be activated in every phase of my life.

Almost is not good enough; I am finishing on top.

Fear will no longer push me to live vicariously through others.

God, I want to be where You have planted me!

Perfection Not Needed

The words I speak will form my life and future.

I will speak what I seek until
I see what I've said.

I am excited about the opportunities that have
entered my life.

All won't be perfect, but I will enjoy the positive
desires of my heart.

*Strive
for progress
not
perfection.*

Life's Lessons

In my life, I have endured trauma.

In my life, I have experienced numerous frustrations.

In my life, I have been attacked by many
negative outside forces.

In my life, I have learned how to live guilt free
through adversity.

In my life, I have made history because
I am still here.

Even in this, I can still smile.

Forget what
hurt you,
but never forget
what it
taught you.

I Am Forgiven

I must forgive so that I can be forgiven.

I will be accountable for my life's mess-ups.

I forgive myself so that I can move beyond:
Mistakes
Failures
Broken relationships
Abusive kinships
Tainted fellowships

My forgiveness has allowed all self-inflicted wounds, hurts, and disappointments to be revoked.

I am forgiven!

Respect

No one has the right to disrespect me.

I will not allow anyone to feel that it's okay to treat me unkindly.

Respect is earned.

I will give respect and expect nothing less.

> WHEN WRITING **THE STORY** OF YOUR LIFE DON'T LET ANYONE ELSE HOLD THE PEN

Bigger Than My Brokenness

I am bigger than my brokenness.

I have experienced many moments that
I deemed as defeat.

During those moments, I realized that I have the
potential to outweigh any brokenness
I have encountered.

I have learned to see beauty in my brokenness.

Life is not measured by the number of *breaths* we take but by the *moments* which take our *breath away*.

Classroom of Life

I will learn the lesson and not live it.

Life will teach me many things, but unfortunately, some will go unlearned.

I have found myself repeating some of the same lessons.

I will strive to learn and ensure my life lessons are not repeated.

GOD Ain't NEVER
HURT ME
IGNORED ME
BETRAYED ME
FORGOTTEN ME
MISTREATED ME
STOP LOVING ME
DISCOURAGED ME

Me, Myself, and I

I will surround myself with people that love me as much as I love myself.

I will be observant of the spirits that I entertain.

I will not allow any negative impartation from outside forces to have access to my life.

Love for myself is beyond others.

love

My Voice Will Be Heard

I was born to speak life or death.

Therefore, I will not lose my voice.

I will use my voice to speak volume to my life.

I will use my voice to encourage, uplift, and empower me and others that are connected to my life.

I Am Not My Past

Gold has a lot of imperfections.

Gold goes through a process of exposing all impurities.

Once the impurities are no longer visible to the naked eye, its value increases.

Gold is not gold until it has endured the purifying process.

This process will determine the value of

real gold over fake gold.

My life has had a lot of imperfections, but to be valued, I must allow myself to go through many processes.

I've learned to know the difference between real and fake.

I will not ignore my past, but I won't dwell there.

My past does not define me; it refines me.

Lifetime Connection

My spiritual life is important.

Therefore, I will connect to the main power source:
Christ Jesus.

I will nurture my inner spirit with the Word of God,
which will direct me in every aspect of my life.

The natural in my life will be governed by
the supernatural.

I will enjoy the favor of God and live in
the overflow.

I will pray without ceasing.

LOVE
keeps me in balance

Change Is the Bomb

Knowing that I have the ability to change is a powerful feeling.

Change is commanding.

Change has the potential to make wrong things right.

Change can be a life adjustment.

Change is the...

Permission Granted

I will tend to myself, rather than waiting on
validation from others.

I give myself permission to...

love others and be loved.

be determined and be stable.

be free of baggage and change.

accept my failures and smile.

be free and be blessed.

be strong and be compassionate.

forgive and be forgiven.

be great and be successful.

love myself and move beyond my past.

live in the overflow.

embrace my accomplishments.

PERMISSION GRANTED

Rollercoaster of Life

My life has encountered ups and downs.

My life has been damaged but not destroyed.

My life has experienced some highs and lows.

My life has not been perfect.

My life has endured hardships.

My life has been subjected to disappointments.

My life has allowed me to cry and smile.

Overall, my life has molded me to become a spectacular and awesome individual.

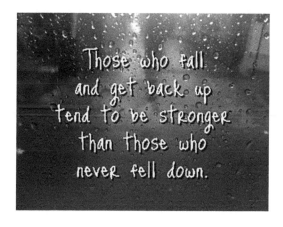

Those who fall
and get back up
tend to be stronger
than those who
never fell down.

Attitude of Gratitude

Look at me now.

I have an attitude of gratitude.

I am grateful for every tear I have cried.

I am grateful for every smile I have smiled.

I am grateful for every shoulder upon which
I am standing.

Thank you to those who went before me and
helped formed my life.

Weapon Power

Isaiah 54:17
No weapon that is formed against thee shall prosper, and every tongue that shall rise against thee in judgement, thou shalt condemn.

In the midst of an emotional war,
I must learn to heal myself.

I have been internally broken.

I have been fighting myself.

I have been trying to figure life out.

No weapon has the power to destroy
what God created.

God, I give You full access to my life.

POWER

My Heart

---

1 Samuel 16:7
The Lord does not see as man sees; for man looks at the outward appearance, but the Lord looks at the heart.

I will allow God to cleanse my heart.

I will accept what God shows me.

I will monitor what my heart harbors.

My heart will no longer feed off negativity.

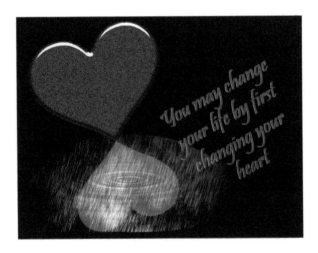

Even after This

I was tried, but I did not lose my mind.

I was tried, but I know in whom I believe.

I was tried, but I still have joy.

I was tried, but my praises to God delivered me.

Even after this, I'm going to experience a mind-blowing, earth-shaking transformation.

I am living for God and myself.

The Need to Purge

Natural purging is an involuntary spasm movement ejected from the mouth.

Spiritual purging is an involuntary spasm movement ejected from the heart.

Purging will free me from impurities and toxins.

My life has been embedded with many things that serve no purpose to me.

Purging cleans out my natural and supernatural being.

Spiritual purging removes unwanted things that I have ingested during my lifetime.

Purging allows God to do His perfect work in me.

Natural purging removes clutter and frees me to enjoy life.

My purging will prepare me for the next level of life.

Bringing It All Together

1 Corinthians 3:6-7
6. I have planted, Apollo watered; but God gave the increase.

7. So then neither is he that planteth anything, neither he that watereth; but God that giveth the increase.

I have acquired what I have because God has allowed me to rest in the blessings that He has bestowed on me.

No man is an island; no man stands alone. Therefore, I need God every step of the way.

My walk with God does not only qualify me to win, but it also makes me a guaranteed winner.

I am a guaranteed survivor.

I am a guaranteed overcomer.

I am a guaranteed warrior.

Move beyond the Break

At times, my peace has been disturbed.

At times, my praise has been limited.

At times, my hope has been hindered.

At times, my joy has been tampered with.

At times, my happiness has been stagnated.

But still, I rise!

I will move beyond the break.

I will change the direction of my life.

I will change my position.

I will change my mindset.

No more giving up.

No more giving out.

Midnight Is Over

Psalm 119:62
At midnight I will rise to give thanks unto
thee because of thy righteous judgements.

Midnight represents the darkest time of life.

Midnight is not all bad, because midnight assures
that daylight and sunlight are nearby.

To move past the midnights of my life, I must learn
to appreciate them.

I must declare that enough is enough.

I will open my mouth and declare, "
This is a new day."

I will open my mouth and declare, "
This is a new beginning."

I will open my mouth and declare, "
This is a new me."

I will open my mouth and declare the
blessings of God.

I will open my mouth and declare my healing.

I will open my mouth and declare my walk
of change.

My midnight is over.

Being Broke Is Not an Option

Colossians 3:1-2
If ye then be risen with Christ seek those things which are above, where Christ sitteth on the right hand of God.

Set your affection on things above, not on things on the earth.

To break is to make a gap or hole in something.

There are many ways of being broke.

My spiritual gage will no longer be broken.

My health will no longer be broken.

My prayer life will no longer be broken.

My heart will not be broken.

My faith will not be broken.

My life will never break again.

My finances will be completely restored.

I am no longer operating in the broken mode, and the blessings of healing will rest upon me.

I Am on the Clock

Ecclesiastes 3:1
To everything there is a season, and a
time to every purpose under the heaven.

Everything in my life has purpose.

I am on the clock that God has laid before me.

My spiritual clock is the only clock that matters.

I may not agree with the happenings of my life,
but I rest assured that my God-ordained clock is
always on time.

Never Again

Genesis 8:21
And the Lord smelled a sweet savour;
and the Lord said in his heart, I will not
again curse the ground anymore for
man's sake.

Never again will I be defeated.

Never again will my name be associated
with shame.

Never again will I lose in life.

Never again will I be left alone.

Never again will I be broke, busted, and disgusted.

Never again will I be in bondage.

Never again will I allow self to take over.

Never again will I doubt the favor of God
upon my life.

I will look at the giants in my life and say,
"Never again."

Power of My Praise

My praise is not to expand my lungs so that
I can simply strengthen my vocal cords.

My praise is not based on my emotional
state of mind.

My praise is not based on the results of my desires.

My praise will not be based on materialistic objects.

My praise is my story.

Every time I praise God, I am telling the world
where I came from and where I am going.

My praise is my narrative.

I am a victor, not a victim.

I Am Who I Say I Am

Proverbs 6:2
Thou art snared with the words of thy mouth; thou are taken with the words of thy mouth.

I will walk in abundance.

I will reclaim my time.

I will not forfeit my blessing.

I will not default on my agreement with the Word of God.

I stand ready to receive my blessings, pressed down, shaken together, and running over.

I will be blessed in the city; I will be blessed in the field.

I will be blessed when I come and when I go.

My faith will enable me to walk in my blessings without seeing them.

Mark 11:23
Whosoever shall say to this mountain, be thou removed, and be thou cast into the sea; and shall not doubt in his heart but shall believe that those things which he saith shall come to pass; he shall have whatsoever he saith.

Change Has Come to Me

Ezekiel 11:19
And I will give them one heart, and I will
put a new spirit within you; and I will
take the stony heart out of their flesh and
will give them a heart of flesh.

I was created with purpose.

My purpose has an assignment.
Others may experience my assignment,
but my experiences will bring change.

No matter how things appear to me,
I must see myself in the future.

I will have the strength to see change.

I have enjoyed things in my life because somebody
stood up and took the initiative to activate change.

I have the power to activate my change.

I have learned to look change directly in the eye.

When looking at me in the mirror, I had to
face reality and get to know myself.

I changed my way of thinking and how
I perceive life.

Five Senses of Life

Sight - Sound - Smell - Taste - Touch

I will see the change; I will hear the change.

I will smell the change; I will speak the change.

I will feel the change.

The change looks good; the change feels good.

I will break the cycle of torment.

I will break the cycle of abuse.

I will break the cycle of loneliness.

I will break the cycle of depression.

I will break the cycle of oppression.

I will break the cycle of a marred reputation.

I will break the cycle of demonic spirits.

My five senses will be strengthened because of
the declarations I have spoken.

A Time of Rededication and Renewal

Proverbs 16:3
Commit thy works unto the Lord, and
thy thoughts shall be established.

Grant me a peace that surpasses all understanding.

Grant me a double portion of praise power.

Grant me a double portion of praying power.

Grant me a double portion of an anointing that
will stay the hand of the enemy.

God, your anointing will cover me.

God, your blood will cover and work in my life daily.

I recognize that You are the source of my strength,
and for that, I give You total praise.

Power of "Re"

Joel 2:25
And I will restore to you the years that
the locust hath eaten, the cankerworm,
and the caterpillar, and the palmerworm,
my great army which I sent among you.

I will live under the ideology of the Power of "Re":

Renew

Reconnect

Rededicate

Refurbish

Restore

Restructure

Redo

Reinforce

Revitalize

Reinvent

Necessary Pain

A child is birthed out of labor pains. Therefore, when pains begin to come, we should know that we are entering the birthing phase.

Good things come from pain.

I will profit from my pain.

I will not have unprofitable pain.

My pain is my process to promotion.

I will not give up in the midst of my pain.

My pain has the power to push me to greatness.

I will not grow weary in my well-doing.

If I don't experience pain amid a situation,
I might be inclined to stay there.

God will take me beyond my pain.

I Speak the Word, and It Is Done

I decree perfection in every area of my life.

I decree wholeness in my body.

I decree soundness in my conscious mind.

I decree wisdom in my financial affairs.

I decree goodwill and forgiveness over any past hurts.

I decree harmony in my house.

I decree prosperity, success, and protection over my life and my family.

I decree perfect love in my God-ordained relationships.

I decree enlightenment and spiritual understanding on my path of growth and maturity.

I decree the peace of God in every area of my life.

I decree new ways of thinking, speaking, feeling, acting, and reacting.

I decree the wisdom to make new choices and the freedom to release from my life those who no longer serve me.

I decree silence to listen to and obey that still, small voice.

I decree a new realization of the presence of God every moment of the day.

I speak the word, and it is done!

I Will

I do solemnly resolve before God to take full responsibility for the choices and actions of my life.

I will love all connected to me, and through my actions as a spiritual being, I will show them the statues of God.

I will confront evil, pursue justice, and love mercy.

I will love God with all my heart, mind, and strength.

I will honor authority and live responsibly.

I will treat others with kindness, respect, and compassion.

I will forgive those who have wronged me and reconcile with those whom I have wronged.

I will walk in integrity and be answerable to God.

I will seek to honor God, obey His Word, and do His will.

I will love myself intentionally and on purpose.

Trust Factor of Life

Proverbs 3:5-6
*[5] Trust in the L*ORD *with all thine heart; and lean not unto thine own understanding.*

[6] In all thy ways acknowledge him, and he shall direct thy paths.

Trust is believing in the integrity, ability, and character of someone or something.

Trust is having confidence beyond what I see or feel.

I trust God.

I trust God's Word.

I trust every word that God has attached to my life.

I trust that my walk will line up with the will and way of God.

My trust has often been challenged, but I have learned not to put my trust in man.

I Am Not My Own

Acts 17:28
For in him we live, and move, and have our being.

My life was bought with a price.

Jesus gave His life so that I would have life.

Jesus shed His blood for me, and I will not allow the shedding of His blood to be in vain.

My actions and thoughts are governed by He who is

Alpha and Omega.

I recognize the importance of believing in God as the power source of my life.

God is the power of attorney over my life.

I exist because of God.

I am the offspring of God.

Equipped by God

2 Corinthians 1:3-4

3. Blessed be God, even the Father of our Lord Jesus Christ, the Father of mercies, and the God of all comfort;

4. Who comforteth us in all our tribulation, that we may be able to comfort them which are in any trouble, by the comfort wherewith we ourselves are comforted of God.

My life is my testimony, and it will bring deliverance to others.

God is my source of comfort, so I have no fear of what comes my way.

I can manage my hard times because I solely depend on God.

As I travel this road called life, God will order my steps.

The hard times of life will mold me into a better person.

I will not live a wasted life.

God has equipped me to go through hard times and come out with a smile.

Live

Psalms 118:17
*I shall not die, but live, and declare the
works of the Lord.*

All that matters is I live.

I am a walking, talking, breathing being
with purpose.

I will not live to exist, but I will exist to live.

No facet of my life will be declared dead.

I command a fresh wind to permeate
my atmosphere.

Psalms 118:18
*The Lord hath chastened me sore: but
He hath not given me over unto death.*

Still, I Rise

Psalms 46:1-3
God is our refuge and strength, an ever-present help in trouble. Therefore, we will not fear.

Knocked down but not knocked out!

Life has suffocated me with situations
and circumstances.

I fell, but God gave me the strength to get back up.

I will not wallow in self-pity.

I will maintain integrity while facing those dark times.

Still, I rise.

I will not let the struggles of life consume me.

Still, I rise.

Every tear I have cried, God bottled it up, and it has
now become my testimony.

Contributors

Thank you for sharing your wisdom and knowledge. I pray that no word written is in vain. I hope every word will take root and enable everyone to love God and themselves.

Pastor Rexsell Hardy

Dr. Tyra Ousley

Anita Riddle

Minister Mojisola Thorpe-Gray

Dr. Jasmine Hardy

Dr. Cassandra L. Simmons

Betty R. Clawson

Pastor Rexsell Hardy works in ministry with his wife at God's House of All Nations. He is known for providing encouragement through idiomatic expressions and thought-provoking statements. Whenever Pastor Hardy is afforded the opportunity to meet people, no one is a stranger to him.

Dr. Tyra Ousley is a servant of the most high God. She is an accomplished educator, clinician, and health care administrator who has experiences ministering in both professional and Christian settings, where she continues to spread the Word of God.

Anita Riddle is an author and creative writer. She has a college degree in Liberal Arts. Her God-given talent has granted her access to many main stages throughout her poetic journey. She has released an audio poetry album entitled *Love: The Road We Must Travel.*

Minister Mojisola Thorpe-Gray is a certified and ordained minister, educator, Christian talk show host, and devotional author. She holds multiple degrees in economics, history, and education. She is passionate about people and their well-being for a prosperous, fulfilled life.

Dr. Jasmine Hardy has a Bachelor of Arts degree in Criminal Justice and a Master's and Doctorate in Clinical Forensic Psychology. She is a staff psychologist with the Department of Justice. Dr. Hardy is a licensed sex offender treatment provider. She is a mentor to many who aspire to have a productive life.

Dr. Cassandra L. Simmons has a Bachelor of Arts degree in Psychology and Sociology and a Master's and Doctorate degree in Clinical Forensic Psychology. She is a licensed sex offender treatment provider. Dr. Simmons is a staff psychologist with the Department of Justice. She is an adjunct faculty member with Grand Canyon University.

Betty R. Clawson was the founding Dean of Dudley Cosmetology University in North Carolina. In September of 1993, she opened the Dudley Beauty College in Chicago. She is a motivational and inspirational speaker. She is the author of *If It Wasn't in You, You Wouldn't See It in Me.*

Mind over Matter

Don't let anybody overpower your mind because they are trying to calculate the power of persuasion.

God's power and wisdom provides the ability to walk away from something you desire and protect what you love.

The mind is a powerful force. It can make the worst of the best or the best of the worst.

Submitted by
Pastor Rexsell Hardy

Everything You Need Is in Your Mouth

Life, as well as death, lies in our words. As kids, we would say, "Sticks and stones may break my bones, but words will never hurt me." Whoever said that was lying. Words hurt! They cause wounds on the inside that may never heal. It's nothing like a stinking wound that smells of past hurts and pains. Long-term wounds cause long-term problems that impact the entire body. People may not know the cause of these wounds, but they can recognize the diseases of self-doubt, insecurity, and lack of confidence.

Often, these wounds begin in our formative years and are repeated over and over throughout our lives. Even when the compliments people give us are genuine, we cannot accept them or, better yet, believe them because we have been told we do not add up, do not fit in, or are not part of the so-called status quo.

Psalms 139:14
I will praise thee; for I am fearfully and wonderfully made: marvellous are thy works; and that my soul knoweth right well.

We are beautifully made in God's image. He made us well, and if He made us well, nothing in our lives is missing or broken. Those words that began in our formative years are disputed by the Word of God.

Submitted by
Dr. Tyra Ousley

My Life – My Choice

I choose me because God chose me.
I reject the pain you inflicted...
Shattering spirits... ill intentions...
Spinning cycles of karma.
Loathing despair through the strength of
spiritual armor.
It's hypocrisy! Falsified rhetoric.
The miscellaneous monotony of memories,
I refuse to let my soul cherish it!
I call you forth, kingdom heir of ingenuity, force
indeed to be reckoned!
Engraved in the Master's hands...in every lasting
remembrance never conformable to second.
Stand in the triumph fought and won for
you this day!
Seek to reverence your God alone.
Humble yourself to pray!
You are divinely defined and refined by the royal
priesthood within which your spirit dwells...
Let your light so shine amongst men,
and in the end, it will be your testimony of
victory they tell.

Submitted by
Anita Riddle

Apple of the Eye

The apple of the eye is the pupil. The pupil is what enables us to see and be seen. If you look straight into someone's eye, you will notice that you can see your reflection in their pupil. This means that you are in the center of that person's focus and they are in yours.

Being the apple of God's eye signifies that you are in the very center of His focus and protection. He loves you no matter what you do or do not do. Just as our sight is valuable to us, you are valuable to Him.

Begin to see yourself as valuable, protected, desirable, wanted, enough, and sought after by the Lord who calls you the Apple of His Eye.

You are the Apple of God's Eye
yes, you!

Submitted by
Minister Mojisola Thorpe-Gray

You Are Important to You

At times, life will render you challenges, uncertainties, and traumas. During these moments, it is necessary to extend yourself grace and understanding.

It's okay to not have answers and just sit in your feelings. It's okay to need time to yourself. It's okay to follow your own pathway to healing and peace of mind.

Humans are gentle yet complex beings. Therefore, we owe it to ourselves to be patient with our unique process of healing and learning. Give yourself the same love and patience that you give others...simply because you deserve it.

There is no better way to deal with life's challenges than to treat yourself to self-care.

This is a beautiful and simple way to tell yourself,

"I love me on purpose."

Self-care can be as simple as drinking tea and sitting in silence or as grand as taking a trip out of the country. You can only be as good to others as you are to yourself, so treat yourself to a nice book, a moment of prayer and meditation, some arts and crafts, or a vacation.

Submitted by
Dr. Jasmine Hardy
Doctor of Forensic Psychology

Fulfilling God's Purpose

God gives each of us gifts to fulfill His purpose.
Are you fulfilling your purpose?
Have you pushed yourself to be your best self?
Are you living or just merely existing?
Have you asked God in prayer what your
calling and gifts are?
If you can't answer these questions, then you have
not done what God has called you to do.

It is your responsibility to discover what gifts you
must use to help someone else along the way.

As you enter your daily journey, reflect upon
these questions and discover what God has called
you to do.

Philippians 4:6-7
Don't fret or worry.

Instead of worrying, pray. Let petitions and praises
shape your worries into prayers, letting God know
your concerns. Before you know it, a sense of God's
wholeness, everything coming together for good,
will come upon you and settle you down. It is
wonderful what happens when Christ displaces
worry at the center of your life.

Submitted by
Dr. Cassandra Simmons
Doctor of Forensic Psychology

Loving Me

If you are living on this earth, there are times when you will need to consume self-love.

When your days, weeks, months, or years seem to be filled with thoughts of what you must do for others, especially if you are neglecting yourself, self-care is your prescription.

When others seem to be progressing and being blessed, you may feel neglected and question your commitment or allegiance. If so, then it is time to examine your self-worth.

The best method of igniting your self-love, invoking self-care, and inspiring your self-worth is committing to memory affirmations that can instantly remind you of who you are and, most importantly, whose you are.

Submitted by
Betty R. Clawson

DECLARATIONS
TO
SPEAK OVER YOUR LIFE

I Declare

I declare that I am strong in the Lord and the power of His might as I put on the whole armor of God and stand against all the wiles of the devil.

I declare that my steps are ordered every day by the Lord.

I declare the favor of God over my life. If God be for me, who can be against me?

I declare that I will delight myself in the Lord and He will give me the desires of my heart.

I declare greater is He that lives in me than he that lives in the world.

I declare that my God will supply all my needs according to His riches in glory by Christ Jesus.

I declare that by His stripes, I am healed.

In closing, what has been established in heaven
shall manifest here on earth.

Remember to say what you want to see.
Everything you need is in your mouth.

Submitted by
Dr. Tyra Ousley

I Am

I am enough.

I am worthy of receiving God-ordained love.

I am not my anxiety.

I am resilient, tenacious, and capable of
conquering any challenge thrown my way.

I am not my trauma.

I am not the negative words that people
have spoken over me.

I am victorious.

I will live a life worth living.

I am a child of God. Therefore,
I am promised a fruitful life.

I am more than enough.

Fear and doubt will not overwhelm me!

Submitted by
Dr. Jasmine Hardy

You Are

You are beautiful.

You are smart.

You are worthy.

You are amazing.

You are kind.

You are important.

Your thoughts matter.

Your feelings matter.

Your story matters.

Our Creator protects you.

Our ancestors are looking over you.

Our elders are praying for you.

Submitted by
Dr. Cassandra Simmons

It's Worth the Effort

Self-Love

God is love, and I am made in His image.
Therefore, I am love.

In other words, loving yourself is an assurance
that you can love others.

Self-Care

Self-care requires excellent health. One of the key
functions of good health is the ability to release
things that have kept you miserable. Often, it is the
inability to forgive hurts and injustices.

It is hard to forgive others when you have
not forgiven yourself.

You must keep growing, or the eternal march of
progress will force you back.

Self-Worth

Whatever you need needs you.

Your assignment is like your fingerprint; only you can
do it, for it belongs only to you.

Learning these nuggets has been a direct result
of my own ups and downs, ins and outs,
and growing from it all.

It's worth the effort.

Betty R. Clawson

May You Have an

Day

I Love Me on Purpose Foundation Summary

This foundation aims to encourage youth and young adults, both men and women, to love themselves unconditionally. The past does not define one's future, but it enables one to grow and glow. The love people have for themselves is not an accident, but on purpose and intentional. I Love me on Purpose has a network of professionals to provide what is needed to aid and assist people to care and love themselves.

Mental Health Specialists

Workshops

Suicide Prevention

Job Fair

Counseling

Financial Planning

Conferences

Mentoring Program

Nutritional Education

Contact Information

Website:
ilovemeonpurpose.com

Email:
ilovemeonpurpose@gmail.com

Facebook / Instagram / Twitter
@ilovemeonpurpose

(833) 756-8363
(833) 7-loveme

About the Author

Dr. La'Vel F. Hardy

Dr. La'Vel F. Hardy was born in Chicago, Illinois. She is an inspirational leader, visionary, motivational speaker, counselor, and teacher who leads with wisdom and grace.

She has undertaken several major projects including overseeing the construction of a multi-million-dollar church and multi-purpose building. She is the President and CEO of I Love Me on Purpose Foundation.

Dr. Hardy teaches on several topics with a focus on helping people to know their worth and value. Her candid communication style allows her to share openly and be transparent about her experiences so that others can apply what she has learned to their own lives. Dr. Hardy so eloquently says, "Everyone is worth every breath they breathe."

She has worked as a social worker with the Department of Human Services, as the Director of Education, and as a teacher at various schools. Little did she know these assignments were merely preparation for a divine purpose in life.

Dr. Hardy's educational accomplishments are:

Associate of Arts Degree
Bachelor of Arts Degree
Master of Science Degree
Awarded the Doctor of Divinity Degree

Dr. Hardy has acquired many certificates. She has served as Executive Director of All Nations Developmental Center and currently serves as the President of All Nations Institute for Learning. She has also served on the Executive Board of E. C. Reems Women's International Ministry.

Dr. Hardy has a personal commitment to family and enjoys spending quality time with her husband, Rexsell Hardy Sr.; their children, Jasmine, Rexsell Jr., and his wife, Tiffany; and grandchildren, Rexsell III and Reign. Dr. Hardy credits her parents and grandmother as the source of her perseverance and sense of self-reliance.

Through her life's experiences and teachings, Dr. Hardy has been afforded many opportunities to inspire individuals in a practical way, through her mandated mission to help transform lives and restore the hurting back to wholeness. She aims to bring healing to individuals and communities.

Dr. Hardy continues to empower, encourage, and enlighten youth, men, and women to love themselves unconditionally.

Dr. La'vel F. Hardy

CPSIA information can be obtained
at www.ICGtesting.com
Printed in the USA
LVHW072245080621
689685LV00013B/1413